COLD DAYS, HOT NIGHTS: THE STORY OF BUDDY HOLLY AND THE CRICKETS BRITISH TOUR

Andrew Johnston

Published in 2018 by FeedARead.com Publishing

A CIP catalogue record for this title is available from the British Library.

Front Cover: Wikimedia Commons
Rear Cover: Author's Collection

For Buddy, Jerry, and Joe. Thanks

About the Author

Andrew Johnston is an academic, currently based at Sheffield Hallam University. A Buddy Holly fan since he was nine years old, he has long been interested in the Rock 'n' Roll era, as well as being a big fan of the music. He lives in Sheffield with his wife and two daughters.

Foreword

This is a project I have had on my mind for a long while; it is part of a continuing quest to write something, anything, on the life of Buddy Holly. The odyssey began in February 1989, the 30th anniversary of Buddy's death. I was nine years old; one Saturday afternoon, my parents had asked me to record a programme on Radio One. It was an hour-long tribute programme, presented by Alan Freeman, called *'Not Fade Away'*. The previous summer, I'd seen the film *'La Bamba'*, so I vaguely knew of the name Buddy Holly.

I remember that afternoon clearly; I was entrusted with a brand-new Memorex C60 tape, one of the predominantly see-through types that seemed to be in fashion then. This one had garish pink, green and yellow swirls and shapes decorating it. Being a diligent nine-year-old boy, I was concerned about missing some of the programme when the tape needed turning over. So, I sat, and I listened to the programme.

I was hooked! I played the tape over and over and over again. The songs were fantastic – and something about their raw simplicity drew me into this music. I needed more, so I went out and bought a record, a greatest hits collection called *'From the Original Master Tapes'*. Then I bought another record, then another. I bought a book about his life, desperate as I was for more information – and, crucially, it had a discography in the back. Now I knew how complete my collection was! I then started collecting the original singles and albums, and then I collected all the bootleg recordings I could get my hands on. I think I have now heard every song, every interview, every preserved live performance, and every fragment that still exist of Buddy's work. And my parents never got that tape.

As the sixtieth anniversary of the Buddy and The Crickets UK tour came around I thought the time was ripe to fulfil my ambitions and write something about it.

This is not *the* story of The Crickets' UK tour but *my* story of the tour. I was not there, I did not witness any of these events. I have, however, listened to as many archive recordings as possible, and there are not many. I've examined the photographic evidence, of which there is plenty. I've read the first-hand accounts of performances; I've been in touch with people who witnessed the tour first hand; and I've read archive publications that gave contemporary accounts of the tour.

From these sources, I have taken the liberty of constructing a narrative of the tour that I feel gives an overview of events as they happened. The events described in this book cover a period just short of one month in the life of Buddy Holly and The Crickets; in that sense it can offer only a snapshot into their lives.

As I said previously, I was not there, but oh boy how I wish I had been …

Tour Map

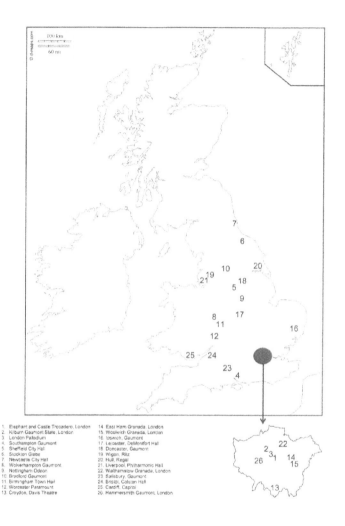

1. Elephant and Castle Trocadero, London
2. Kilburn Gaumont State, London
3. London Palladium
4. Southampton Gaumont
5. Sheffield City Hall
6. Stockton Globe
7. Newcastle City Hall
8. Wolverhampton Gaumont
9. Nottingham Odeon
10. Bradford Gaumont
11. Birmingham Town Hall
12. Worcester Paramount
13. Croydon, Davis Theatre
14. East Ham Granada, London
15. Woolwich Granada, London
16. Ipswich, Gaumont
17. Leicester, DeMontfort Hall
18. Doncaster, Gaumont
19. Wigan, Ritz
20. Hull, Regal
21. Liverpool, Philharmonic Hall
22. Walthamstow Granada, London
23. Salisbury, Gaumont
24. Bristol, Colston Hall
25. Cardiff, Capitol
26. Hammersmith Gaumont, London

Tour Itinerary

Date	Location	Venue
1st March 1958	London	Elephant and Castle Trocadero
2nd March 1958	London	Kilburn Gaumont State
3rd March 1958	Southampton	Gaumont
4th March 1958	Sheffield	City Hall
5th March 1958	Stockton	Globe
6th March 1958	Newcastle	City Hall
7th March 1958	Wolverhampton	Gaumont
8th March 1958	Nottingham	Odeon
9th March 1958	Bradford	Gaumont
10th March 1958	Birmingham	Town Hall
11th March 1958	Worcester	Paramount
12th March 1958	Croydon	Davis Theatre
13th March 1958	London	East Ham Granada
14th March 1958	London	Woolwich Granada
15th March 1958	Ipswich	Gaumont
16th March 1958	Leicester	DeMontfort Hall
17th March 1958	Doncaster	Gaumont
18th March 1958	Wigan	Ritz
19th March 1958	Hull	Regal
20th March 1958	Liverpool	Philharmonic Hall
21st March 1958	London	Walthamstow Granada
22nd March 1958	Salisbury	Gaumont
23rd March 1958	Bristol	Colston Hall
24th March 1958	Cardiff	Capitol
25th March 1958	London	Hammersmith Gaumont

Chapter One – That'll Be The Day

"... this is rock n roll like we've never heard it before in Britain!"
[Keith Goodwin, New Musical Express]

March 1958 was cold, unusually cold. The arrival of Spring seemed to be forever delayed as Britain remained in winter's grip. Flying into this frigid climate were Buddy Holly and The Crickets, for whom Saturday the 1st of March marked the beginning of their 25 date UK tour. Having landed at Heathrow Airport (then known merely as London Airport) two days previously the group were unprepared for the weather that met them. They had begun the week on tour in Florida, and the contrast could not be more apparent; their stylish, but thin, leatherette jackets offered barely any protection from the elements, even with them zipped right up under their chins. In front of them was a gruelling journey of nearly two thousand miles up and down the trunk roads of England and (briefly) Wales to play fifty-five shows, as well as three television appearances, and at least one radio spot.

The tour was eagerly anticipated by The Crickets' British fans. *'That'll Be the Day'*, had topped the British charts the previous autumn, and by the turn of the year the group had collectively scored a further two top 10 hits with *'Oh Boy'*, and *'Peggy Sue'*. Even once sales had begun to fall, and the records began to slip down the charts, they remained high in the jukebox most played lists, as British teenagers kept on playing them in youth clubs and coffee bars across the country. As quickly as the group had appeared on the horizon, rumours of a British tour began to surface.

Also fuelling the anticipation was the fact that Britain, while gripped by the same rock n roll craze, had not been exposed to many live appearances by American rock n roll acts at the time. Bill Haley's February 1957 tour, and Charlie Gracie's visit the following August represented the only appearances by US acts in Britain thus far. The Crickets, in a sense, were pioneers; not only were they popular, but they were one of the first acts that British audiences could see and hear in person at a time when such appearances were rare. As a result, they captured the imagination of many British teenagers, with their influence keenly felt by some who went on to define the music scene of the following decade.

Foremost amongst their followers were John Lennon and Paul McCartney; "We did practically everything he put out" Lennon later enthused. "What he did with '3' chords made a songwriter out of me!! He was the first guy I ever saw with a capo. He made it OK to wear glasses! I WAS Buddy Holly"[1]. These sentiments were also echoed by McCartney; "He wore glasses, and you didn't see anyone with glasses. It seemed that anyone with glasses couldn't make it as a singer". Holly also inspired the pair to begin writing their own songs. While Lennon and McCartney did not manage to see the tour, they both saw the television performance on the popular variety show '*Sunday Night at the London Palladium*'. A number of future performers did, however, manage to see the show, including: Joe Cocker, Mick Jagger, Mike Pender, and Alvin Stardust.

It seems almost incredible that such a following had been developed from so little exposure. The Crickets' success was based on just these three records, six songs in total. And these record releases were their only exposure in Britain. This, though, was not unusual for the time. Television was not the international medium it is today; therefore, British audiences had not been able to see any of The Crickets' appearances on US Television. In terms of radio, the BBC was the sole operator at the time, and they did not feature much in the way of rock 'n' roll music. Radio Luxembourg offered more hope of hearing the latest hits but was generally only heard clearly after dark. No videos accompanied the record releases as they do today. The main way for fans to see their favourite stars performing their songs was via the plethora of rock 'n' roll films that had appeared in the cinemas; for example, *'The Girl Can't Help It'* (which featured Fats Domino, Little Richard, Eddie Cochran, Gene Vincent, and The Platters), *'Rock Around the Clock'* (which featured Bill Haley and the Comets, The Platters, and Freddie Bell and the Bell Boys), *'Rock, Rock, Rock'* (which featured Connie Francis, Chuck Berry, Frankie Lymon and the Teenagers, and LaVern Baker) or *'Don't Knock the Rock'* (with Bill Haley and Little Richard). However, none of these featured The Crickets.

What this tour did achieve was to positively shower a wealth of new material on the British fans. Firstly, two new singles, '*Listen to Me*' and '*Maybe Baby*', saw their release literally as The Crickets arrived in London, and were followed by the mid-March release of their debut album '*The Chirping Crickets*'. It must have felt, during that long cold month of March that the floodgates had opened; fans could buy more recordings, they could see the group on television, and they could see them in person. Oh Boy!

Front Cover of the Tour Programme *(author's collection)*

Chapter Two – Tell Me How[2]

"If I was to go back to the dawning of it all, I guess I'd have to start with Buddy Holly."

[Bob Dylan, 2016 Nobel Laureate Speech]

Bob Dylan's acknowledgement of the influence of Buddy Holly on his development as a musician and songwriter in his Nobel Prize acceptance speech neatly highlights the regard in which he is held in the music community.

In some ways Buddy Holly was an unlikely rock 'n' roll star, in other ways, he was the quintessential rock 'n' roll star. He was an unlikely star in that he didn't look like a rock 'n' roll star; Elvis was all coiffed hair and dark eyes; Gene Vincent was menacingly cool in his black leather; and Little Richard was a frantic mass of big hair and big eyes. Buddy wore glasses. He was also tall and skinny, his long limbs did not lend themselves easily to suggestive dance moves, and his dark curly hair did not lend itself easily to the classic ducktail hairstyle of the era. He knew he would never capture the Elvis look; Jerry Allison remembered that "no regular person looked or dressed like Elvis. It was beyond their reach and we looked like the boys next door"[3]. For Buddy Holly *it was about the music.*

The importance of Buddy Holly as an artist stems from the fact he was a singer-songwriter *and* instrumentalist. In this, though, he was not the first; both country music and the blues have a long history of singer-songwriter-performers. Artists such as Hank Williams and Chuck Berry also sang, played guitar, and wrote their own songs. It was more about the songs themselves, which provided blueprints to all the budding musicians out there with easy to use chords, bright melodies, straightforward song structures (typically following A-B-A-Solo-A-B-A-Coda or A-A-B-Solo-A-A-B-Coda patterns), the basic band structure of lead/rhythm/bass guitars and drums, and harmonised backing vocals. His music was innovative; the recordings stand out through their use of techniques such as double tracking, and the use of echo chambers, different instruments, and strings to produce a range of different sounds and textures. Yet, while they may have followed a similar blueprint, each was unique.

Music was in Buddy's blood. He was born on the seventh of September 1936 in Lubbock Texas, into a family where most played an instrument or sang. From an early age his prowess was evident, first through playing the piano and later on the guitar. When he started High School, Buddy became friends with Bob Montgomery, who shared his interest in guitars. The two of them quickly developed a double act, Buddy and Bob, playing country and bluegrass music together. They also started writing their own songs, following in the footsteps of their hero Hank Williams. The duo was popular, playing small gigs in and around Lubbock as well as live shows on the local station, KDAV.

Early in 1955, Buddy and Bob were the opening act for a show featuring Elvis Presley. This encounter changed his entire musical focus, for now Buddy wanted to play rock 'n' roll music, just like Elvis. By the time Elvis returned to Lubbock in June, Buddy was a fully-fledged rock 'n' roller.

By the time Buddy Holly and The Crickets arrived in Britain in March 1958, they had been a regular presence in the record charts for around six months. Their first single *'That'll Be the Day'* had reached number one in both the US and the UK. They quickly proved they were no one hit wonders, following up with rock 'n' roll classics *'Oh Boy'* and *'Peggy Sue'* in the Autumn of 1957.

The Crickets' chart success had arisen since they joined up with their producer/manager, Norman Petty, in February 1957. Petty was the owner of the NorVaJak Studio in Clovis, New Mexico, located around one hour's drive North west of their home town of Lubbock. Holly began using Petty's studio to record from early in 1956. At that time, Buddy was signed to Decca records, for whom he eventually undertook three recording sessions in Nashville that yielded two unsuccessful singles. Unsurprisingly, given the absence of a hit record, Decca were not keen to maintain their relationship with Holly, and opted not to take up their option on his contract for another year.

Holly, while disappointed, did not give up. He was frustrated with the set-up at Decca; in Buddy's opinion, producer Owen Bradley did not seem to understand the sounds he heard in his head, nor the way his records should sound. This is apparent in the recordings themselves. While some can be considered good performances, for example '*Blue Days, Black Nights*' and '*Rock Around with Ollie Vee*' have stood the test of time and stand up as fine rockabilly recordings, on other cuts, Buddy seems to be trying to be something he is not. Too often the delivery is too 'breathy', as if he is straining to perfect the timbre of the song; yet the result often feels a bit disjointed. This leaves the feeling that he is singing at least one key too high on a lot of these songs. This is clear on the first version of '*That'll be the Day*', a song Buddy had originally written in the summer of 1956 after seeing the film 'The Searchers' in which John Wayne's character, Ethan Edwards, repeatedly uses the phrase as a put-down. While it is not that far from the later version, it still feels quite raw, as if unfinished, and drowned in so much echo that the vocal almost sounds like a call and response.

The experience left Holly wanting more control over his recordings; he was the songwriter, guitarist, and the vocalist. As the creative force behind these songs, he needed a better way of transferring the sound in his head onto tape and needed to work with someone who understood what he heard. He also wanted to play with his own band; at Decca they had been reluctant to let him record with his own musicians, Jerry Allison on drums, Don Guess on bass, and Sonny Curtis on lead guitar.

In Petty, Buddy found someone who was happy to let artists record at their own pace, charging by the session rather than an hourly rate, preferring instead to recoup costs via a percentage of the song's publishing rights. He was also independent of the record companies and had an ear for a well-engineered recording. Throughout 1956, while still contracted to Decca, Buddy had held a number of demo sessions in Clovis, ostensibly to see what his compositions would sound like if they were produced his way. He quickly realised Petty's approach allowed him the creative freedom to do this and was receptive to the suggestions Petty made in order to get the best sound possible on the recordings.

Keen to put his experience at Decca behind him, Buddy was not giving up. He felt that '*That'll Be the Day*', still had potential, *if only he could get it to sound right*. Norman Petty was happy to support this, and in return for a percentage of the song's publishing rights, he promised to use his industry contacts to get the record released. The only problem was that under the terms of his Decca contract, Buddy was forbidden from re-recording anything he had already recorded for them. Despite pleas to the contrary, Decca held firm.

Undeterred, in February 1957 Buddy went ahead and re-recorded *'That'll be the day'*. Accompanying him into the studio was a different set of personnel from his previous session; Jerry Allison remained on drums, but Larry Welborn was now on bass, and Niki Sullivan was recruited to play rhythm guitar. In order to hide his presence on the recording from Decca, Buddy decided to hide inside a group. Casting about for names based on an insect theme, and having discarded the name 'The Beetles', they settled on The Crickets.

Through his connections with the music publishing firm, Southern Music, Norman Petty managed to get the group signed with Brunswick Records (ironically a Decca subsidiary)[4]. *'That'll Be the Day'* was released at the end of May 1957, steadily gaining radio play and sales over the summer until it reached number one on the chart in late September. That same month, the record was released in Britain, topping the chart in November.

Throughout the spring and summer of 1957, while *'That'll Be the Day'* was making its progress up the charts, Buddy and The Crickets had been busy in the studio. Under Petty's supervision, they had recorded a wealth of material, including some of their most well-known songs such as: *'Words of Love'*, *'Not Fade Away'*, *'Everyday'*, *'Oh Boy'*, and *'Peggy Sue'*. There had, however, been a small change in the composition of the group as Larry Welborn had decided not to remain with the group and was replaced by Joe Mauldin.

As soon as *'That'll Be the Day'* had begun to break across the US, The Crickets were in demand to play live shows. They toured with Clyde McPhatter in August before joining the 'Biggest Show of Stars' tour, featuring a roll call of classic rock 'n' roll acts such as Chuck Berry, Paul Anka, The Drifters, Frankie Lymon, LaVern Baker, and The Everly Brothers. Beforehand, they made their first appearance on national television on American Bandstand, where they performed their latest hit. The tour then kept them busy for weeks, playing a series of one-night stands from the beginning of September to the end of November.

The prolific writing and recording period over the summer of 1957 led Brunswick to propose a novel solution to prevent a backlog of material waiting for release, and possibly to cash in while the group was successful. They proposed releasing some of these recordings on another subsidiary, Coral, under the name Buddy Holly, while continuing to release others by The Crickets.

Under this new arrangement, two new releases hit the stores in the autumn of 1957; *'Peggy Sue'*, credited to Buddy Holly, and *'Oh Boy'* credited to The Crickets (both of which featured the same personnel, although Crickets records featured added backing vocals, whereas these were mostly absent on Buddy Holly releases). In Britain, however, all records were released on the Coral label.

By December, with the tour finished, The Crickets again appeared on national television, this time as guests on Ed Sullivan's show. It was after this that Niki Sullivan decided he wanted to leave the band as his personality clashed with Jerry's, which had resulted in a physical fight, and he was also tired of the non-stop touring.

After a brief break for Christmas it was off to New York's Paramount Theatre for a two-week engagement with 'Alan Freed's Christmas Show of Stars' that began on Boxing Day, and also featured Fats Domino, Jerry Lee Lewis, Danny and The Juniors, The Everly Brothers, and Paul Anka. While they were in New York, the group appeared again on national television, performing *'Peggy Sue'* on Arthur Murray's Dance Party.

Their engagement in New York finished on 6th January. Just two days later they set off on yet another tour with their close friends, the Everly Brothers. Once this engagement was completed, The Crickets embarked on their first overseas tour, to Australia with Jerry Lee Lewis and Paul Anka where they played a total of eleven shows. After stopping en route to play a show in Hawaii, they finally returned home on 9th February. By late February, they were again on the road, this time for a six-day tour of Florida that finished on the 25th. Two days later they flew out of New York, bound for London.

Birmingham Town Hall *(Wikimedia Commons)*

Sheffield City Hall *(Wikimedia Commons)*

Chapter Three – Oh Boy!

They're Here! The Rocking, chirping Crickets … are in Britain for their first concert tour!

[New Musical Express, Friday 28th February 1958]

BOAC Flight 582 transported Buddy Holly and the Crickets into London on the cold Thursday afternoon of the 27th February 1958. With them were their manager Norman Petty and his wife Vi. For some, it was headline news; the British music press, teenage rock 'n' roll fans across the country, as well as the group and their entourage themselves had all been eagerly anticipating the visit. While The Crickets had spent the past few weeks performing in Hawaii, Australia, and Florida, they were still excited to visit Britain. As Jerry Allison later remembered with a chuckle, "when we came to England, we had fans everywhere!"[5] After nearly six months of nearly non-stop touring, they were by now used to their fame, as well as being recognised by their fans, but in Britain the group felt that their fans were keener, and their admiration was somehow more intense.

Keen to capture the scene for posterity, Norman Petty documented the approach of their propeller powered Bristol Britannia aircraft into London (the transatlantic jet age would not begin until September of 1958) with his new, colour, cine camera. Filming as they descended through the clouds, he captured the group's first glimpses of the country from the air. It was not particularly impressive; 1950s London was a grey and drab looking place, a low-rise cityscape bisected by an equally grey looking River Thames, which wound lazily through its middle. Once the aircraft was safely on the ground and its four propellers had shuddered to a halt opposite the squat brown brick and glass facade of the single terminal, then known simply as the Europa Building, the party were able to disembark into the frigid air where they were met by their driver for the next few weeks, Wally Stewart, a bald-headed middle-aged man in a long raincoat.

London, and, for that matter, Britain, was a very different place in 1958 to today. Despite then Prime Minister Harold MacMillan's assertion the previous year that the population had 'never had it so good' with respect to living standards, the country was only slowly shaking off its post-war malaise. Rationing, introduced on the outbreak of war in 1939, had finally ended only four years previously. The economy was growing, boosted by increased employment in manufacturing sectors as well as the increasing productivity of workers in this sector. And the population were indeed feeling the benefits of this growth, as wages had been growing by over seven percent per annum since the beginning of the decade, although by 1958 this had begun to slow.

The economic structure of the country to an extent determined its appearance. Visitors to British towns and cities would be met with a vista of tall chimneys and smoky skies, particularly in the industrial heartlands of the Midlands, North, Wales, and Scotland. There were still over half a million miners working in collieries across the country, mining the coal that powered the economy, blackened the atmosphere, and stained the buildings.

1950s Britain would also have felt larger due to transport and communication constraints. Fewer people owned cars; there were around five million registered in 1958, compared with over thirty million in 2018. There was also less capacity on the roads, there were no motorways, nor were there many dual carriageways or bypasses. Britain's first stretch of motorway, the eight-mile Preston Bypass, was not opened until December 1958, followed by the southern section of the M1 the next year. Most long-distance journeys would have involved driving on single carriageway roads, which passed through the centre of every town and city en route.

Railways were still predominantly steam operated, with the journey from London to Edinburgh taking around eight hours. British Rail's modernisation plan, introduced in 1955, committed to the replacement of steam by diesel and electric trains, a change that only began to gather momentum in the following decade. Air travel was the preserve of the rich and famous only.

There were also only two television channels in 1958, the state operated BBC and the commercial ITV. The BBC's 'toddlers' truce', where the station did not broadcast between six and seven o'clock in the evening so that parents could put their children to bed, had only ended in 1957. Although by 1958, for the first time, a majority of households owned a television set. In contrast, only around ten percent of households had a telephone.

Politically, this was a country whose influence was waning. Britain had been stung by the failure of the Suez War in the Autumn of 1956, an ill-judged attempt to seize control of the canal. The cherished Empire was declining as independence movements grew up in the colonies and new countries were formed as British rule retreated. Despite pretentions to the contrary, it was clear that the remainder of the Twentieth Century would see world events shaped by the opposing superpowers of the USA and USSR. This was the Britain that was to be The Crickets' home for the next three and a half weeks.

Their first destination was the Cumberland Hotel, Marble Arch, whose seven-storey brick edifice overlooked the famous landmark at the entrance to Hyde Park, providing the group with the perfect base for that weekend's activities[6]. Saturday's opening performances were to take place at the Trocadero Cinema, Elephant and Castle, which was around four miles to the south of the hotel. The second night of the tour was scheduled for the Gaumont in Kilburn, which was a similar distance to the north. Travelling times were especially important that Sunday as, scheduled in between the two Kilburn shows, was a television appearance at the London Palladium, which would involve a soundcheck there, then a tip to Kilburn, back into London for the Palladium show and then back to Kilburn for their second set.

"They're here!" announced that week's New Musical Express (NME), confirming the band's arrival. However, the event probably needed little in the way of an announcement as music fans had been well informed of The Crickets' impending arrival. Just days after the group's work permits were secured from the Ministry of Labour and National Service (they were valid for five weeks from landing), the first stories of their upcoming visit began to appear.

The basic tour itinerary was revealed by the NME to their readers on 7th February, outlining the first few dates plus the news that the tour would include at least two television appearances while they were in the country. The Daily Mirror briefly mentioned the upcoming tour to its readers a few days later, including news that the group would appear on Jack Hylton's TV show, 'See you Soho' on Thursday 27th February, which was broadcast only in the London region on the local ITV franchise. By the final week of February, Disc Magazine, which had only begun publishing a few weeks previously, was reporting to its readers the growing excitement about The Crickets' arrival, enhanced by the publication of the full list of dates and venues so that fans were now aware of where they could see the show. In the following issue, published on the very eve of their arrival, Disc announced an appearance on the *'Cool for Cats'* TV show on the evening of their arrival in Britain, usurping the previous plan to appear on the London only 'See You Soho' programme.

The *'Cool for Cats'* television show represented the first time anyone in Britain would have been able to see The Crickets perform. Presented by Kent Walton, who also presented a show of the same name on Radio Luxembourg, *'Cool for Cats'* was one of the first TV programmes to showcase rock 'n' roll in Britain. Broadcast on Thursday evenings at 7:30 pm from Wembley Studios in north-west London, the show ran for just 15 minutes on the ITV network. Indicative of the breathless pace of the next few weeks, The Crickets would have had very little time to get accustomed to their new surroundings before they were back in their car for the twenty-minute drive to the TV studios in North West London. As no footage of recordings have survived, coupled with an absence of reports from the media, it is hard to judge anything about this appearance. As such, it appears to have been a very low-key British debut for the group, who merely mimed to their latest release, *'I'm Gonna Love You Too'*, which had reached the shops that very day.

Friday 28th February marked The Crickets' first full day in Britain. It was a busy day, mainly taken up by a press reception at the Whisky A-Go-Go club, located in the Soho district of London, around a mile from their base at the Cumberland Hotel. The reception had been arranged by the Decca Record Company, of which the Crickets' Coral label was a subsidiary. In order to generate some publicity, the promoters had decided that a photo opportunity featuring The Crickets with actual cricket players would work well. Consequently, a rather bemused looking Godfrey Evans, the Kent and England Wicketkeeper, and the recently retired batsman Denis Compton were invited along to the reception. Aged thirty-seven and thirty-nine respectively, they were unlikely to have been fans of rock 'n' roll, but the two parties appear to get along, with the five men appearing to be chatting amiably in the photos taken that day.

These moments were captured by photographer Bill Francis, the twenty-seven-year-old founder of the Flair Photography studio, based just a short distance from the Whisky A-Go-Go on Wardour Street. Francis' black and white photos capture the smiling Crickets, who were easily identifiable as a band through their matching cream sweaters, posing with the suited Evans and Compton. They all appear to be enjoying themselves; the photos show them good naturedly engaging in a game of cricket; the cricketers showing The Crickets how to hold a bat, and how to position themselves behind the stumps as if fielding. Forty years later, Compton recalled their meeting fondly, describing Holly as a 'nice chap', although he remembered the meeting taking place at Lord's Cricket Ground[7].

After posing with the sportsmen, the three Crickets moved on to speak with the female journalists sent along by Valentine Magazine. Bill Francis' photos capture the good-natured horseplay between the five of them; with Buddy and Jerry first waltzing two of the reporters around the room before lifting them onto their backs, in the style of a fireman's lift, and twirling them around Texas style. There were smiles all around, the band impressing with their warmness and sense of fun, clearly feeling uninhibited enough to mess around with their guests.

The tour was different to anything the Crickets had experienced at this point in their careers. They were the headline act of a two-hour show that featured an orchestra, other singers, and a comedian. As Joe Mauldin later remembered "we were the rock 'n' roll act on a variety show, and I thought that was the deal over here [Britain], that people wanted to see a variety show rather than straight rock 'n' roll". While this may have been a new departure for The Crickets, this was a typical format of tour packages in 1950's Britain. Bill Haley had toured the previous year in a package that also included an orchestra, other non-rock n roll singers and even Desmond Lane on the tin whistle! Similarly, Charlie Gracie shared the bill with jugglers and a ventriloquist on his tour. Early British Rock n Roll acts followed the same pattern in their first tours; Terry Dene, Tommy Steele, and Lonnie Donegan all toured on mixed bills throughout 1957, while one of Cliff Richard's early tours saw him supported by 'trick cyclists' 'stilt dancing puppeteers' as well as Harry Bailey 'the King of Blarney'.

Sharing the bill with The Crickets were thirty-two-year-old Ronnie Keene and his orchestra, described somewhat enthusiastically as 'Britain's new musical sensation' on the tour posters. A piano player from his early years, Keene had been called up by the Army in

1944 and spent two years playing with the Royal Artillery Band. His professional break had come two years after he left the services, joining the Ken Macintosh Band and adding the saxophone and clarinet to his repertoire. After working with a number of other acts, he went solo as a band leader in 1955, playing dates around the world, on BBC programmes, and appearing on film with Frankie Vaughan in *'These Dangerous Years'*. His swept back hair, topping a thin but longish face, accented by a pointed chin and sharp nose, gave Keene something of the look of a matinee idol, particularly with the formal black suit and bow tie that formed his stage outfit. The orchestra was accompanied by singer, Lynne Adams, who performed vocal duties when required[8].

Next on the bill were Stella and Frances Tanner, two sisters in their early thirties who had been performing together since the beginning of the 1950s. They had enjoyed some success with their closely harmonised renditions of songs such as *'Rag Mop'* and *'Green Door'*. They were reasonably well known to British audiences through their appearances with the Hedley Ward Trio on the *'Educating Archie'* radio show in the early 1950s. With their dark curly hair cut into stylishly short bobs, high cheekbones, and pointed noses that gave their faces an elegant look, the sisters cut sophisticated figures in their sparkly off the shoulder dresses.

The line-up was completed by singer Gary Miller. He was, in early 1958, signed to Pye Records, having achieved a top ten hit with *'Robin Hood'* in late 1956. He is probably better known today for providing the singing voice for the character Troy Tempest in the children's' TV show *'Stingray'* and his rendition of the song *'Aqua Marina'* which played over the programme's closing credits. However, in 1958, was enjoying a run in the charts with songs such as *'The Yellow Rose of Texas'*, *'Garden of Eden'*; and *'The Story of My Life'*. His round face, topped by a crop of fair hair, which was swept back from a left sided parting gave him a boyish charm, slightly reducing the formality of his on-stage attire of dark suit and bow tie. His suntanned appearance on the tour was the result of spending a number of weeks in Cyprus playing to servicemen.

The show was compered by twenty-six-year-old Des O'Connor. Smartly dressed in his dark suit and neatly combed hair, which seemed to belie his smiley features and laid-back style, the tour's poster billed him as 'The Comedian with the Modern Style'. His job was to keep the show moving as compere, link man, comedian, and singer. While O'Connor became a well-known star of British television in the following decades, in 1958 he was plying his trade on the variety circuit. As such, the tour represented a significant opportunity for him, he later recalled how the money he earned had enabled him to buy his first car. It was also his first exposure to rock 'n' roll; "I'd never seen amps before so it was sensational, so exciting to see the beginning of something new," he remembered later[9].

Buddy made a favourable impression on his co-stars, many of whom later recalled their time with him fondly. Des O'Connor remembered him as a "real sweet, fun guy"[10] While the contrast between the frenzied reception received by the Crickets to the distinctly cooler reception he received from the audience led Ronnie Keene to the realisation that "it was all over for musicians like me". Despite fearing for his future career, Keene still found Buddy to be "a lovely lad. There were no big star affectations about him at all. He used to talk to the boys in my band as if he was one of them"[11]. The two band leaders would sit next to one another on the tour bus, sharing their stories, talking about their music, and looking at the landmarks as they passed by. Photos from the rehearsal suggest a deep mutual respect existed between performers from the very beginning of the tour, capturing Keene, Holly, and Miller, all in their stage outfits, studiously looking at Keene's sheet music and deep in conversation.

Coulston Hall, Bristol *(Wikimedia Commons)*

Posters from the tour (Author's Collection)

Chapter Four – Rave On

"Wherever they may be playing, I am confident that these ambassadors of song can be assured of a rapturous reception."

[New Musical Express, February 1958]

The tour proper began on Saturday 1st March. The itinerary saw the performers generally booked to play traditional style cinemas, which had generally been built in the 1930s in the art-deco style and housed between two and three thousand patrons, doubling as live venues when not showing films. Occasionally, they played a dedicated live venue in cities such as Sheffield, Newcastle, Birmingham, Liverpool, and Bristol. They played two shows per day, the first generally starting between 6:00pm and 6:30pm and the second at 8:30pm. On Saturdays an additional 2:30pm matinee show was added. Tickets, as for all shows on the tour, cost six and a half shillings (32.5p) and ten and a half shillings (52.5p).

Prior to the first show, a full rehearsal took place at that night's venue, the Trocadero cinema, Elephant and Castle. Located just south of the River Thames on the busy New Kent Road, this 'super cinema' dated from 1930 and could seat up to three and a half thousand patrons, and also housed a Wurlitzer organ reputed to be the largest ever shipped to Europe at that time. The afternoon rehearsal explains the lack of an early matinee on this afternoon, the only Saturday on the tour where this happened. Photographer Bill Francis was again there, following up his previous day's work at the Whiskey a Go Go, this time accompanied by another photographer Phillip Gotlob who also captured the days' activities[12].

Their pictures capture the performers mixing happily, chatting with one another, maybe swapping stories, as well as joking and fooling around. The Crickets appear to be chatting amiably with the other performers and joking amongst themselves. In between times, the band performed their songs. Buddy, pictured with Stratocaster in hand, appears to be giving a full-throated performance as Gotlob's frame captures him mid song. The only discernible difference between rehearsal and actual performance is their stage attire, Buddy performing the rehearsal wearing a warm looking ribbed jumper instead of the long drape jackets and bow ties that characterised the Crickets' stage outfits.

While backstage, Buddy was interviewed by Bill Holden for Melody Maker, which described The Crickets as 'one of the breeziest packages to be imported into Britain'. The journalist, however, found Buddy to be 'very cautious', apparently taken aback by his rather pessimistic attitude towards the longevity of the rock n roll craze; "We've been going a year," Buddy told him, "and one always wonders how long it's going to last. But so far, the public seems to like us, and we hope that as long as we don't make any mistakes we shall be alright."

This concern about mistakes probably refers to the fact that this was the first time the group would play an elongated set list on tour. It may also have been a tactic designed to deflect criticism, with many interviewers asking him questions around how long rock n roll would last, it may have felt to Buddy that the best answer was to wonder along with them.

The first show began at 6:30pm. For fans of The Crickets, it was a long wait to see the band; the show was opened by the orchestra. Des O'Connor's first appearance followed, providing a short link segment before introducing The Tanner Sisters. Gary Miller then ended the first half of the show.

Following a short interval, the beginning of the second half saw the return of the Ronnie Keene Orchestra, playing a recognisable tune, at least in the eyes of the teenage segment of the audience, the theme from *Six-Five Special'*, which was the BBC's then year old foray into a television programme showcasing rock 'n' roll music. Des O'Connor then began his final segment, which consisted of him singing a number of standards such as *'Put Your Arms Around Me'*, *'Shine on Harvest Moon'* as well as his version of latest hits such as *'At the Hop'*. Once he'd finished his final skit, he would then introduce the final act with a wave of his hands, announcing to the crowd "ladies and gentlemen, Buddy Holly and the Crickets".

Audiences went wild for The Crickets; throughout the tour, the venues would erupt with the sounds of clapping and cheering as soon as they were announced. The shows that night at the Elephant and

Castle Trocadero were, by all accounts, well received, with their twenty-minute set based on their hit singles to date. According to Melody Maker, the audience for the first show was around fifteen hundred, which doubled for the second, despite the attraction of Elvis Presley's latest film, *'Jailhouse Rock'*, playing at the local cinema.

Their performance began with *'Everyday'*, followed with what were described as 'ear shattering versions' of *'That'll Be The Day'*, *'Peggy Sue'*, *'Oh Boy'*, and *'Maybe Baby'*. They also threw in a number of covers, two by Little Richard that were staples of their act *'Rip It Up'* and *'Ready Teddy'*, and Gene Vincent's *'Be Bop A Lula'*. To Ronnie Keene, who was first on stage that night, it was obvious that the audience were not there to see his orchestra; "we were just the cannon-fodder" he recalled. "Still, we weren't booed: they listened to us and clapped politely".[13] The only hint of negativity was in respect to Buddy's stage movements, where reviewers were less than kind about his ability to match the stage moves of Elvis.

Reviews were, on the whole, positive. Disc Magazine described the Crickets as "not perhaps the best … but certainly the noisiest", citing Holly's guitar and vocals as doling out 'the sledgehammer treatment', delivering a high tempo, ear-splitting performance. The other artists were generally commended, Gary Miller's 'dignified yet dynamic performance' was highlighted, as well as the efficiency of the Ronnie Keene orchestra, the precision of the Tanner Sisters, as well as the personal success of Des O'Connor achieved despite 'a slow-ish start'.

Most reports highlighted the sheer noise the three Crickets were able to generate, leading some to label the performances 'the loudest rock show yet!' As well as the loudness of the show, the group's ability to recreate the sound of their records was also praised. The other members of the troupe shared the media's fascination with their amplified sound. Yet, in reality this consisted solely of Buddy's fifty-watt amp, as Joe's bass and Jerry's drums were both un-miked, although as Ronnie Keene recalled, they were still noisier than his entire orchestra

The tour was now underway, and so began an unremitting schedule. There was, however, no time to stop and reflect on a successful opening night as Sunday 2nd March was a particularly busy day. First, The Crickets faced two shows at the Gaumont in Kilburn (6:30pm and 8:30pm), while in between their Kilburn performances they were to headline the popular '*Sunday Night at the London Palladium*' TV show, broadcast between eight and nine o'clock that night. The programme was one of the most popular on the fledgling ITV network, and had been broadcast live from the famous Argyle Street venue in the heart of London's West End since the channel's launch in 1955. It was basically an hour-long variety show that featured an eclectic mix of entertainment, not unlike the tour they were on, as well as the popular 'beat the clock' segment, which involved the completion of a host of zany challenges in return for prizes.

'*Sunday Night at the London Palladium*' was produced by ATV, whose head, Lew Grade, was also the promoter of the concert tour. The appearance had been confirmed at the beginning of February through a flurry of telegrams between Grade and Norman Petty, guaranteeing nationwide exposure for the group.

However, the Crickets' first priority was to travel to Kilburn's Gaumont cinema, which sat astride the busy High Road, part of the A5 that stretched from central London to the port of Holyhead in Wales. As the Gaumont was only around three miles from their central London base, it would have only taken around fifteen minutes to travel there. The cinema itself was built in the art deco style, with a tall white central tower (supposedly designed to evoke the Empire State Building) that allowed its glowing red sign to be seen as it shone out above the terrace of shops that lined the main road. Prior to arriving there, the band visited the London Palladium to sound check for that night's TV appearance, performing a quick run through to ensure microphone and camera placings were finalised. The highlight though for the group was the fact they got to meet Bob Hope, who breezily shouted an exaggerated "how are you boys?" by way of a greeting as he walked past. According to Jerry Alison, "he was about as bigger deal as you could get in the United States," and the star struck band managed to respond with "fine Mr Hope."[14]

That evening, the band took to the stage in Kilburn following Des O'Connor's final link segment. Sporting their dark grey suits, black bow ties, and white shirts they again filled the venue with sound of rock 'n' roll, to the delight of the assembled crowd, and despite the fact that Buddy managed to break a guitar string while playing. Once they had finished their set, they had to rush straight into their car, where Wally was waiting to drive them straight down the A5, into the

West End to the Palladium. From there the three Crickets went straight into their dressing room and waited nervously until their cue.

That night's broadcast was the one hundredth edition of the show; headlining along with The Crickets was the aforementioned Bob Hope, as well as ballerina Alicia Markov, who was dancing a special routine accompanied by the John Tiller Girls and the London Palladium Orchestra. Comparing the show was Robert Morely, who also introduced the 'Beat The Clock' segment, which always brought a certain level of anarchy and unpredictability to the show. It appears that The Crickets arrived at the Palladium amid all the confusion of *'Beat the Clock,'* as Buddy later wrote to his parents that he'd appeared on a show with that name.

Around 8:30pm that Sunday night, the wider British public got their long-awaited glimpse of Buddy Holly and The Crickets on the television. As the golden curtains opened, the revolving stage deposited the band into the frame and right into the middle of millions of TV screens. They stood slightly to the right of the centre of the stage, Buddy in the middle, Joe to the audience's left with his stand-up bass angled inwards towards him, and Jerry to the right crouched over his drum kit. As the audience applause died away, three quick kicks on the bass drum announced their first number, *'Oh Boy'*! Immediately the band were on the money as they not only filled the auditorium with the sound of Rock 'n' roll, but, more importantly, delivered their music into living rooms across the country.

As Buddy sang, the camera panned in to a close up of his face, with his famous black horn rimmed, almost oversized, glasses filling the screen as he went into the second verse of the song. And they sounded just like they did on record; the songs were driven by the jangling notes from Buddy's Fender, accompanied by a pounding drum beat from Jerry, and underpinned by Joe's subtle bass notes. Of course, the only difference was that the songs were performed with no backing vocals.

It was Buddy who drove the performance; as he reached his first solo he adopted the now familiar pose, leaning back with his right leg straight and his left leg bent, head bent forward as he looked down on the fretboard of the guitar and began the solo. He then drew back towards Jerry, his long legs stretching out as he went to work on his Stratocaster with a fast and furious solo. Once they had finished the song, the show took a commercial break.

The programme resumed to the jangling introduction to *'That'll Be the Day'*, again closely following the recorded version, again minus any backing vocals, but with a note perfect solo. Then, two stomps on the bass drum introduced the pounding beginning to their final number, *'Peggy Sue'*, and then it was over. He spoke not a word, other than a brief thank you; there was no short interview with the host as there had been on the Ed Sullivan Show. Yet, what he communicated was immense. Here they were, a self-contained band, playing their own songs, on their own instruments.[15]

You cannot help but think that the final segment of the show featuring Bob Hope came too soon for the majority of music fans that Sunday night. His wry observational humour, quick one-liners, and showmanship were all very well, but for the fans of the Crickets, the performance came and went. For the Crickets themselves, there was no time to ponder the performance, nor even to catch Bob Hope's segment, as they were due back in Kilburn to perform their second set.

They made it back and performed as planned, with the audience also being treated to an extra half an hour of music on the theatre organ by Norman Petty, who had found the instrument and decided to give it a whirl. According to Buddy, if Vi Petty had joined her husband at the keyboard they could have been there all night!

Keyed up after a busy day, sleep was the last thing on the band's mind as they headed back to their hotel. Throughout the day, Buddy, Jerry and Joe had been engaged in a discussion around cars with the NME's Keith Goodwin and Allan Crawford of Southern Music, the group's publishers. Their debate centred around which was the best sports car available; Holly himself was torn between a Jaguar and a Mercedes, Allison favoured an MG, and Mauldin an Austin Healey. As they drove back, someone suggested that the best way to settle the argument was to see the cars in the flesh, so at 2:00am the party of five were driving around the deserted streets of London looking for car showrooms to inspect their wares. Every time they reached another showroom, Buddy hopped out to look after first opening the doors for the rest to follow.

Keith Goodwin enjoyed his time with The Crickets, joining them again at the end of the tour once they reached London. He was just a year older than Buddy, which encouraged a rapport between him and the band. Goodwin remembered him as "a very nice, easy-going lad", although his habit of answering his questions with a 'yes, sir' or 'no, sir' made him feel like there was a certain level of deference towards him, much to his frustration. Goodwin also picked up on Holly's restlessness. "He would never relax", he recalled, "he wanted to see places and get a feel of a town by walking around". This restlessness meant that after a performance Buddy was up into the early hours and was therefore reluctant to get up the next morning. Des O'Connor remembered being frequently deputised to fetch Buddy each morning, tugging on his legs in order to get him out of bed, which was met with the response "don't pull my legs Des, I'm tall enough already"[16].

After the previous night's events, the 8:00am start that Monday would not have sat well with Buddy. That morning, the performers boarded their tour bus and headed south-west out of London to the City of Southampton, roughly two hours' drive down the A3, to perform two shows at the Gaumont cinema. The show there was again well received, with a sizable proportion of the audience made up of sailors from the nearby naval base. Instead of staying in Southampton for the night, The Crickets headed back to their London hotel, arriving around 2:00am. Despite the lack of sleep over the last few days, and probably still feeling the effects of jet-lag, and the cold, Buddy could not sleep. Instead of sleeping he sat in his room and wrote a letter to his parents detailing the events of the weekend.

The following day, the tour party began a daunting one-hundred-and-seventy-mile trip north to Sheffield, around five hours travelling time in these pre-motorway days. On the way, The Crickets made a quick stop in Chesterfield, a town located just over 13 miles to the south of the Sheffield. The group had a walk around the town centre, where Buddy was pictured as he and Vi Petty walked through the deserted Marketplace (which was only occupied Thursday-Saturday), with the long since disappeared Cathedral Vaults pub in the background. It was still cold. Buddy's long leather coat was zipped right up against the elements; Joe Mauldin followed behind with his matching coat similarly fastened to the top, while a few local shoppers go about their business oblivious as to who they are passing.

They reached Sheffield later that afternoon, checking into the Grand Hotel for their overnight stay. They later emerged into the rain to walk across to the City Hall, the venue for their two shows that day, stopping to get directions from Tony Land, who was passing at the time. Buddy breezily asked, "Hey big fella, which way is it to the City

Hall?" Land pointed out the landmark to the group, to which Buddy replied "thanks, big fella" and went on his way, only recognising who he had just spoken to as he walked off. He was probably more familiar with the sound rather than the sight of The Crickets, as he had actually purchased tickets for that night's show!

Their performances in Sheffield were well received. Despite the fact it was a variety show, the audience were mainly there for The Crickets. Sixteen-year-old Chris Fox later recalled, "everybody just wanted to see Buddy Holly. He was very exciting. He was all over the stage. On TV he would stand in one place [but] the concert was electrifying." Fresh from his earlier encounter, Tony Land also enjoyed the show, remembering that "the sound from his Fender Stratocaster was awesome, especially when he played Peggy Sue." Also in the audience that night was Joe Cocker, although he was less impressed with the performance, later on recalling that he had preferred Jerry Lee Lewis' performance a few months later.

Yet, the majority of fans were satisfied. Seventeen-year-old Cliff Hircock labelled it "a cracking show". He was also impressed by their sound, "there were just three of them on stage and the sound was incredible. You got the sound of the record. Looking back, I have wondered how they did it. The amplification in those days was so basic but it worked. Everybody had a heck of a time."[17]

Following the show, Hircock decided to get a closer look of the group and wait around and try to speak with them. As the minutes ticked by, and feeling colder by the minute, he decided that he'd had enough and headed for the bus stop a few streets away to travel home. He was only just rounding the back of the building when he literally ran straight into the three Crickets as they left the venue. "We stood and chatted for quite a while. They did a lot of travelling and had just done two shows at the City Hall and it was late. The guy must have been out on his feet, but he was happy to stand and natter for more or less as long as we wanted."

The tour then headed to the North East of England, performing two shows in both Stockton (Globe) and Newcastle (City Hall), before returning to the Midlands on Friday for two shows in Wolverhampton (Gaumont), followed by another two in Nottingham (Odeon) on Saturday. Prior to the performances in Wolverhampton, the band were interviewed on the 'Bright Lights Show', a radio programme hosted by Leslie Dunn and broadcast by the Midlands Home Service on Friday afternoons. They had been on the programme before, appearing via a tape they had sent over bearing a message and a brief jingle. The host was seemingly excited to get the group into the studio, albeit for a very brief conversation, his clipped tones offset by the more exotic sounding Texas drawl of his guests, exemplified by Buddy politely prefacing his answers with a 'yes, sir'. [18]

The interview began with a gentle ribbing from Dunn as to how they had pronounced Birmingham on their tape (Bir-ming-haam, with the emphasis on the middle syllable), prompting Buddy to laughingly protest "well, we didn't know, you know, and we still don't know quite how to pronounce it, cos the lingo is pretty hard to get down to at times". He then explained to the listeners that the group were in the country until the 25th, before running through the outline of their next US tour. Asked by Dunn if they had any plans for making films he replied, "No sir, we don't have any plans, er, just exactly definite plans. We've had a couple of offers for some films, but we haven't accepted them as yet".

Dunn then brought up the media reports complaining about the lack of backing vocals from the Crickets, with Buddy politely explaining that they are an instrumental group but that they do sing on stage. When asked about the naming of the group, Buddy demurs to his drummer, saying "well, Jerry, the drum player, thought of that" who then interjects with an explanation that "there's quite a few crickets, the insect crickets, in Texas".

And that was the end of the interview, save for one last question asking which of the records they wish to play next. "Well, there's two of 'em", Buddy replied, quickly getting in a plug, "The Crickets and then the Buddy Holly record. I think the side, 'Listen to Me', is the one that is considered to be going in the States now; I'm not sure which is going best here". After a polite round of thanks, the interview concludes with Dunn giving '*Listen to Me*' a spin.

The tour played three shows in Nottingham's Odeon Cinema on the Saturday, where Buddy later recalled it "snowed like mad", before Sunday night's shows in Bradford completed the first week of the tour, which had by now covered over six hundred miles. However, compared with the distances they were used to travelling on their US tours, the group did not consider this as onerous. In a column for the NME, Buddy told his fans that they saw "journeys from two-hundred to three-hundred miles as 'short-hops' … so you see, the journeys we are making between dates in Britain are really small and aren't any bother to us". He was probably also enjoying the camaraderie of the tour bus, spending his travel time talking music with Ronnie Keene, or telling stories or jokes with Des O'Connor. Des later remembered that they did a lot of shopping wherever they went, The Crickets no doubt wanting to spend some of their money on mementos of their trip.

Holly's fellow performers also remembered his openness towards them and fondness for talking. They were, on the whole, enjoying themselves. Buddy was particularly impressed with both the reception from and behaviour of the fans. "They're always very receptive and make us feel right at home" he told the NME. "They listen while we're playing, don't scream and holler out, and then reward you at the end with good, hearty applause". He was also impressed by the technical setup of the venues they played, and complimentary of all the backstage personnel the group had encountered, including stagehands, stage managers and electricians. And while the group had reservations about performing a twenty-five-minute set, compared with just two or three songs on their previous tours, Buddy was pleased with the way they had successfully elongated their set to eight or nine songs.

Prior to the Bradford shows, the group spent the afternoon at the cinema watching the film '*Bridge on the River Kwai*', which was currently on general release in the UK. That Sunday night, the Bradford audience gave the Crickets their usual rapturous reception. However, local critic, Peter Holdsworth of the Bradford Telegraph and Argus, was less than impressed. Beginning with an assumption that the audience were merely thrill seekers looking for the latest gimmick or novelty, his review slated the performance of "this foot-stamping, knee falling musician." Holdsworth's main problem seemed to stem from the fact that he could only understand around a quarter of the words Holly was singing, accusing the musicians of distorting their talent in order to win the audiences favour. Then, clearly signposting to his readers that he was not a rock 'n' roll fan in the slightest, Holdsworth signed off by asking his readers "where on earth is show business heading?"

Chapter Five – Everyday

"British disc spinners get double value for their money with the current visit of the American group, Buddy Holly and the Crickets."
[Melody Maker, March 8th, 1958]

The second week of the tour began with the performers embarking on a two-hour journey from Bradford south to Birmingham, where two shows at the Town Hall were scheduled. On route to Birmingham, The Crickets' party made a detour to visit the vast Longbridge car plant[19]. Built in 1905 by the Austin Motor Company, the factory had been through several extensions in the intervening years, and was, in 1958, the home of the British Motor Corporation, which had been formed through the merger of Austin with Morris Motors in 1952. Being huge car fans, The Crickets' were keen to have a chance to tour what was the home of British car manufacturing. No doubt, the previous week's discussion regarding the best sports car was resumed, with Joe doubly excited as he could now see his favoured Austin Healey actually being built!

On arrival, the group, accompanied by Norman Petty, were met by two BMC apprentices, Dennis Hill and Des Kellaher, who showed them around the factory. After being introduced to their guests, one of them struck up conversation with Buddy with the question "Mr Holly, what do you do for a living?" clearly oblivious as to whom the guests were. After a tour of the production lines and workshops, the group posed for photographs on the front steps that led down from the entrance of the Art Deco building, their matching cream sweaters gleaming in the afternoon sunshine. Their tour guides then joined them for a picture on the steps, the all-round smiles suggesting they had all had enjoyed themselves[20]. Buddy later wrote that the group had got "quite a big kick" from the factory visit and were particularly impressed by the fact they got to see the whole factory "going right from the foundries to the assembly rooms".

After leaving the factory, The Crickets were driven into the centre of Birmingham for the first of their shows. The Town Hall was, and still is, an impressive venue with its stone columns lining the building on all sides in the classical style, designed to mimic a Greek or Roman temple. Once inside the venue, the band would have seen the building's other distinctive feature, the large organ, whose pipes reached up from floor to ceiling at one end of the building[21].

It was an impressive sight for those who were there that night, although the group seemed so small against the backdrop of the huge organ pipes and tall columns. Photos from that night show Buddy in his long drape jacket leaning back from his microphone to play a solo, Jerry in the background hidden by his drumkit, surrounded on all sides by the audience. In Birmingham they also added a cover of Jerry Lee Lewis' *'Great Balls of Fire'* to their set, which was well received by the fans.

Tuesday evening saw the tour play Worcester, which, being only twenty miles south of Birmingham, made it the shortest distance between venues since they had left London the previous week. They played two shows at the Paramount, another Art Deco style cinema located in the middle of town.

Pat Mace, then a teenage shop assistant, had been waiting for this day for weeks. She lived in the nearby village of Evesham, and once she knew that the Crickets were coming to play in Worcester, she was eager to see them in person. "I heard That'll be the Day by Buddy Holly and the Crickets and absolutely loved it. When we heard they were to play a concert in Worcester as part of a British tour, a group of us got together and travelled there by train."[22]

After the show, she decided to seek out the group in the hope of getting an autograph from one of them, remembering later that she "left the others in the foyer of the theatre and went around the back to the stage door. I was amazed to find the only person there was a member of the Gaumont staff and the door was open." She got more than she bargained for as suddenly Buddy appeared and asked her what she wanted. When she asked him for an autograph, he was more than happy to oblige, "come on in" he said, and she followed him to his dressing room, where she encountered Jerry and Joe relaxing after the show while they played Little Richard records.

After around forty-five minutes in the dressing room, their driver Wally shouted that they were ready to go. Pat took the cue to leave, as she did Buddy asked for her telephone number, which she was only too happy to give. He promised to call her, a promise she didn't take that seriously; she was just excited to have seen the group, and even meet them in person afterwards.

For the Crickets, a hundred-mile journey back to London beckoned, returning to their original base at Marble Arch. Over the next three days they played six shows in and around the capital: firstly, Croydon on the Wednesday, followed by two shows in East Ham on the Thursday, and Woolwich on the Friday, where a fourteen-year-old schoolboy from nearby Dartford, Mick Jagger, caught the show.

Buddy, restless to see more of London, and possibly frustrated about the lack of something to do while on the tour bus, had decided to buy an acoustic guitar to play on his travels. So, Des O'Connor took him to Denmark Street in Soho, a street famous for its musical instrument shops. The comedian recalled that Buddy "went into a music shop and must have tried about seventeen guitars. They all sounded the same to me, but he picked up a Hofner, said it had a good tone and bought it"[23]. While they were back in London, The Crickets had the opportunity to meet Lonnie Donegan, one of Britain's leading exponents of skiffle who had notched up six top ten hits by early 1958, including two number ones. Keith Goodwin of the NME arranged for the musicians to meet on Friday afternoon, where according to Donegan they indulged in the stereotypically British pastime of drinking tea together.

They quickly hit it off; Donegan was impressed with Holly's Fender Stratocaster, remembering "he was the first person to bring a solid guitar into the country". He was also impressed with the Jerry's drumming as he'd "never seen a drummer like Jerry Allison before. He was all over his kit. It was great Texas drumming". Their friendship established, The Crickets were invited by Donegan to a concert in aid of the American blues singer Big Bill Broonzy at the Dominion Theatre, where Donegan himself was performing along with jazz musicians Chris Barber and Ken Coyler. Once their final show in Woolwich had finished, Wally drove them the eleven miles back into central London in time for the midnight start. Buddy later shared his admiration for Donegan with his fans, writing in the NME "we like your Lonnie Donegan real good", noting that it was also the first time he had seen 'Dixieland bands' playing live, and that while that kind of music was not to his taste, he thought they played 'real well'.

During this second week of the tour that the group's latest record releases entered the British charts for the first time. According to the *Record Mirror*, disc sales were surging; '*Listen to Me*' lead the way, as Buddy had predicted on the *Bright Lights Show* a few days earlier, charting at sixteen, while '*Maybe Baby*' had entered slightly lower at number twenty-eight. With '*Oh Boy*' still at number nine and '*Peggy Sue*' at nineteen, the group now occupied four places of the top thirty.

Despite its promising chart debut, and Buddy's confidence in the release, '*Listen to Me*' was not as well received by the critics as his previous discs. Don Nichol, reviewing for '*Disc*' magazine, felt that it was not up to the standard of '*Peggy Sue*' and that the 'B' side, '*I'm a Gonna Love You Too*' was the likelier hit. However, there was very little time to reflect on either these achievements or criticisms, as Saturday morning saw the troupe on the road once more and bound for Ipswich, where they were due to give their customary three shows. Before they left London, however, Buddy had fulfilled the promise he made to Pat in Worcester to get in touch by phoning her at work to invite her to come to London the following week to catch the final show of the tour in Hammersmith. She readily agreed.

Two weeks of non-stop travel was by now beginning to take its toll on Buddy. Despite his cheerful insistence the previous week that the travelling was no problem, he was feeling the effects of life on the road. He had developed a cold and was growing tired of the cold weather, wondering aloud in a postcard to his sister whether it could ever get warm in Britain. No doubt the long hours on the tour bus plus the late nights and busy itinerary were not helping his mood, but the enthusiastic reception the band received in each venue would have cheered him up. Even if he was beginning to feel jaded, the performances showed no sign of flagging.

Buddy began the performance by telling the audience "it's good to be here in …" pausing with dramatic effect to ask Jerry and Joe where they were, who in turn shouted "Ipswich!" Bryan Knights was there that Saturday, sitting in awe as the "three men filled the Gaumont with sound. [However], there was no sophisticated amplification or lighting system. The big man Jerry Allison sat behind what in these days would be called a mini-drum kit, little Joe B Mauldin slapped a double bass that seemed to be twice the size of him, while Buddy himself produced remarkable sounds from his Fender

Broadcaster [sic] and sang in that by now so familiar voice, with every word clearly audible." After the show, Bryan joined the ever-growing list of lucky fans who were able to meet the group, get an autograph and have a quick word with them.[24]

En route to Sunday's shows in Leicester's DeMontfort Hall, The Crickets stopped off in Cambridge to see the historic university town and break up their hundred-mile journey. The group had a brief walk around the city centre, stopping by the River Cam to examine the punts from Magdalene Bridge, in the shadow of the college of the same name. As they stood there in the spring sunshine, Norman Petty took up position on the other side of the road to again capture the scene on his cine camera. A short piece of film captures the group looking over the bridge, hesitantly turning around to see if Petty is still filming and turning hastily back when they see that he is.

Petty's film also captured a few minutes of the arduous road journey between performances, with the coach slowly winding its way along a twisting trunk round, which, of course, was a single carriageway. It is unlikely that they were able to average much more than forty miles per hour on these journeys. In addition, there were few places to stop in between towns for refreshments and breaks, which would have made the journeys seem longer.

Two New Releases: *'Maybe Baby'* and *'Listen to Me'* (author's collection)

'The "Chirping" Crickets' Album *(author's collection)*

Chapter Six – Words of Love

"This American tune team are certainly celebrating their visit to Britain with a surge of disc sales"
[Record Mirror, 14th March 1958]

The third week of the tour began in Doncaster with two shows at the Gaumont cinema. That Monday night, a fifteen-year-old schoolboy named Bernard Jewry, caught the bus from nearby Mansfield to see the performance, bringing along his guitar. He managed to talk his way back stage, soon encountering Buddy who, seeing his guitar, invited him to play. As he started to play Jerry and Joe fell in behind as he strummed the chords to *'Peggy Sue'*. Thoroughly pleased with having been able to not only meet but also to play with The Crickets, Jewry was also able to make himself a lasting memento of the encounter by persuading the three performers to etch their autographs into his guitar. Within three years Jewry had begun a music career of his own, first assuming the name Shane Fenton and charting a number of records in the top thirty. In the early 1970s he assumed a new name, going to on to greater success as Alvin Stardust.[25]

This third week saw The Crickets and their fellow performers travelling back and forth over the Pennines, the hills that form a spine across the middle of Northern England. From Doncaster they travelled west to Wigan, returning the next day to the east coast for two shows in Hull before retracing their steps to the west for two shows in Liverpool.

Tuesday 18th March saw the troupe perform in Wigan at the Ritz Cinema, a last-minute replacement for Blackburn where the show was apparently cancelled due to lack of ticket sales. On the way to Wigan, The Crickets' party had stopped in Manchester where Norman and Vi Petty bought some high-quality worsted wool to be shipped back to New Mexico. Once again, the fans enjoyed the show. Sixteen-year-old Barrie Critchley was there that night. "The crowd went wild," he recalled, "they had never heard music like that before".[26]

While in Wigan, The Crickets stayed at the Grand Hotel. On checking in, the group encountered Barbara Bullough behind the hotel's reception desk. As she was familiar with both American customs and American English from her parents' frequent trips to the US, she quickly impressed the group by using American terms, such as sidewalk instead of pavement. A rapport quickly developed with the group, and Buddy was particularly taken with her. He spent the afternoon persuading her to attend the show, insisting she must come. She agreed, and he arranged the tickets for her for that night.

Barbara was impressed with their performance. "I had no idea about Rock 'n' Roll - I was brought up on classical music - but I thought the show was wonderful" she remembered. After the show Buddy accompanied her home by taxi, as she had missed her last bus home. They shared a kiss outside her home, then Buddy surprised her by asking her to stay with him for the next week while he completed the tour. She had to refuse; "I knew my father would never stand for something like that, so I had to say no". Instead she agreed to come and see him again when he played Liverpool the day after next.[27]

They checked out their hotel the next morning and headed for Hull and two shows at the Regal Cinema, which marked the twentieth stop on the tour. Buddy said his goodbyes to Barbara, who presented the group with their bill on which she and fellow receptionist, Jo, had written 'oh boy' next to each of The Crickets' names. Buddy was keen to remind her about her promise to see him again in Liverpool just "tell them you're Barbara from Wigan and they'll let you in," he told her as he bade her farewell.

The journey from Wigan to Hull and back to Liverpool added a further two hundred miles to their trip. Barbara kept her promise to attend the show. She told the door staff who she was and managed to catch up with Buddy backstage, but to both their frustration she had to leave before the performance began to return to Wigan. She missed a show that was interrupted by technical hitches. The first show was not well attended, with only three hundred reportedly in attendance, which meant that two-thirds of the stalls were empty.[28]

The size of the audience did not prevent an excited welcome from the fans; the band came bounding onto the stage to a big cheer from the crowd. Yet, after plugging his guitar into his amp, no sound came out. After a few attempts to use other jacks, Wally Stewart was summoned to have a look. The Crickets trooped off dejectedly to be replaced by Des O'Connor, who attempted to keep the audience occupied while fuses and plugs were changed on the amp.

Finally, after forty minutes, the fault was fixed, much to Des O'Connor's relief as he desperately tried to keep the audience entertained and distracted, while running out of material. Back came The Crickets and they launched into their set. After a couple of songs, the problems and delays were well and truly forgotten by all. Launching into *'Oh Boy'* the band began to ratchet up the theatrics; Joe alternated between riding his bass and playing it while laying down next to it, with Buddy jumping around the stage next to him. In between songs he told the audience how much he liked playing in England and how much fun he'd had meeting so many fans.

The second show was smoother. The delay meant that the second audience had begun to queue outside while the band were still on stage, being treated to a sample of what was to come. Mike Pender, founder member of The Searchers, was there that night; he remembered it as a "magical night. It was music hall acts really, but Holly had his Fender Strat and there were just the three of them on the stage. It was still a big sound and loud, and the audience was on its feet. It was fantastic." The audience was larger for the second show, and the reception just as ecstatic. By their final number, a cover of *'Ready Teddy,'* Buddy had even taken to playing his guitar behind his head. At the end of the show, Jerry threw his drumsticks into the crowd.

Curiously absent that night were The Beatles. Despite being huge fans of The Crickets, not one of them saw the show while they were actually in their hometown. It has been speculated that the reason for this is that they could not afford it, but, as Mark Lewisohn notes, the cheapest ticket would have been within their reach. More likely is that the offer of a paid performance of their own, at the newly opened Morgue Skiffle club, was too good to turn down and the real reason they stayed away.[29]

From Liverpool it was back to London, and another night at the Cumberland Hotel. It was a busy Friday; their first stop was the BBC's Riverside Studios rehearsing and recording a performance for the *'Off The Record'* TV show. Located in Hammersmith, West London, a few hundred metres from the banks of the Thames and next to the sprawling Charing Cross Hospital complex, the studios had been acquired the previous year by the BBC. At this time the studio was home to shows such as the popular comedy *'Hancock's Half Hour'*, which was broadcast live from the premises prior to the adoption of tele-recording.

Presented by Tony Payne, *'Off the Record'* was a thirty-minute show that was broadcast on Thursday evenings at 7:30pm. The band's segment, which involved miming to their recording of *'Maybe Baby,'* was recorded and was due to appear in the following week's show.

This record was, by now, clearly the bigger hit of the two recently released records, with sales having pushed it up to number fourteen on the charts for the week ending 15th March, on its way to a peak of number four, while *'Listen to Me'* had stalled at number fifteen. Yet, while the fans were not buying the discs in equal numbers, they were certainly playing them both on jukeboxes around the country, as that week each featured in the top ten of the jukebox charts.

Their recording commitments with the BBC fulfilled, The Crickets then headed for the Walthamstow Granada for two shows that night. They received a warm reception from the crowd, and an ovation at the end of the show, which led the local reviewer to comment that "this young American vocal team will stay in the top ten for years to come". They writer was impressed with their presentation, noting Buddy's 'strangely shaped electric guitar'; although noted that despite the fans' reaction the group did not have time to perform an encore.

Chapter Seven – Listen to Me

"Everyone comments on how my jokes get bigger laughs than the comedian on the show, Des O'Connor. Who knows, we might change and be comedians instead of rock n roll stars"

[Buddy's letter to parents, 22nd March 1958]

The remainder of the tour involved shows in the West Country and Wales. Saturday 22nd March saw the troupe headed west out of London for three shows at the Gaumont in Salisbury, roughly eighty miles away. The Crickets stayed at the Old George Hotel, which dated from the Fourteenth Century, and was described by Buddy as 'a real, old, quaint place' in a letter to his parents he posted from the town. After the additional matinee show had finished, Norman Petty decided to film the comings and goings in the town, while Buddy and Jerry went shopping. They were spotted by Diane Fishlock who recalled that "my friend and I were in Woolworths before attending the early evening concert when we saw Buddy and Jerry Allison. We just followed them round, watching as they purchased some pens, managed to get their autographs and had a short chat".[30]

In between shows the group also had afternoon tea at their hotel, gathering around a large table in the traditionally decorated restaurant, complete with roaring fire. Afterwards, Buddy followed his now familiar routine of chatting up the hotel's receptionist, this time engaging Margot Warrender in conversation, then offering her free tickets for the last show of the evening. Margot was slightly bemused at the attention, "I wasn't really a rock 'n' roll fan and must admit I didn't really know who Buddy Holly was," she remembered.

Buddy wrote that he was pleased with all three shows, and that the final one was the best they had performed all tour. He felt they had now perfected playing a twenty-five-minute set, as well as their onstage antics, and he'd even thrown in some jokes from Des O'Connor, which, he bragged to his parents, were getting much bigger laughs from the audience. Although, from the comedian's point of view, it was his laconic delivery and Texas accent that made the jokes sound funnier.

From Salisbury, the tour continued west to play two shows in Bristol's Colston Hall on Sunday 23rd March and then another two shows at the Capitol Cinema Cardiff on Monday (which, incidentally, was the day Elvis Presley was inducted into the US Army). It has long been rumoured that Neil Kinnock, the future politician and Labour Party leader, attended one of the Cardiff shows. However, while he was a big fan, he was not there.[31]

On Tuesday morning, it was back to London for the final time, one last night in the Cumberland Hotel, and their final performances at the Hammersmith Gaumont (now the Apollo). The first Hammersmith show was marred by an amplifier problem, which was soon fixed by Norman Petty. After sorting the problem, Petty was able to capture some film of the second show. The brief colour segment captures the Crickets sprinting onto the stage, Buddy with his lightweight fender across his middle, followed by Joe who is lugging his large bass beside him, while Jerry sprints through the orchestra to the drum kit. The next frames show Buddy bopping up and down on the spot as he sings into the microphone, strumming furiously at the strings of his Stratocaster. Petty's film also captures their on-stage antics, with Buddy and Joe facing each other on stage, Joe lowering himself backwards until he is lying on the ground playing the double bass that was by now practically laying on top of him, while Buddy is on his knees, simultaneously leaning backwards as his guitar waggles as he plays.

In between performances, however, some boisterousness had managed to get out of hand. Joe had produced a cigar to celebrate the end of the tour, which he then lit and began blowing the smoke around the dressing room, much to the annoyance of Buddy and Jerry. A scuffle soon broke out, good naturedly at first, as they tried to separate Joe from his cigar and put it out. It quickly escalated into more of a brawl as the three of them grappled with one another, the end result was Joe managed to headbutt Buddy in the mouth, knocking the caps off his two front teeth. So, for the final show Buddy had to resort to smearing chewing gum across his remaining teeth to hide the gap.

Their performances over, thoughts began to turn towards travelling home. The group were due to fly out of London the following day so had little time for packing and goodbyes. Buddy

48

gave his new Hofner guitar to Des O'Connor as a present, which the comedian gratefully accepted.[32] Their performances done, and while they relaxed in their dressing room, the NME's Keith Goodwin, who had once again re-joined them in London, asked the group if they'd enjoyed themselves. Buddy grinned and replied "sure, we had a real ball! It was just great!" Sitting across the other side of the dressing room, Jerry and Joe nodded their agreement. Over the course of twenty-five nights, fifty-two shows, two thousand miles of travel, and around one hundred thousand satisfied patrons, so had Britain.

Insert from Tour Programme *(author's collection)*

Epilogue – Not Fade Away

"Now it can never happen, but Buddy Holly package show was coming here …"

[New Musical Express, 6th February 1959]

A little more than ten months after leaving Britain, Buddy Holly was dead. He, along with Richie Valens and the Big Bopper, plus pilot Roger Peterson, were killed in a plane crash while on tour in Iowa in February 1959. He was twenty-two years old.

In those ten months Buddy's life had continued at a frantic pace. On their return to the US, The Crickets joined Alan Freed's Big Beat Show, a tour that began on 28th March 1958 just two days after their return from Britain. The tour wound its way around the US from New England to the South West, via The Midwest and back again, finishing on the 9th May. By the end of May the group had returned to Clovis to record for the first time since February, cutting *'It's So Easy'*, and *'Lonesome Tears'* which appeared as a single in September 1958, along with the enduring classic *'Heartbeat'*. A few days later, Holly returned with a different backing band to record demos of two songs he had written with his first singing partner Bob Montgomery *'Wishing'* and *'Love's Made a Fool of You'*, intended to be offered to the Everly Brothers in due course.

June found the band making promotional visits around the US. Following this, Buddy headed to New York to meet executives at his publisher, Southern Music. It was there he first encountered Maria Elena Santiago who worked on the reception desk. Taken by her Latin beauty and sophisticated manner, Buddy soon got talking to her, persuading her to go out with him that evening. While they were out that evening he proposed. They were married in Lubbock on 14th August, 1958.

While in New York, Buddy fitted in a recording session, minus the other Crickets, to cut both sides of his new solo single *'Early in the Morning'* and *'Now We're One'*. The first two weeks of July were taken up with a two-week tour of the Midwest for the *'Summer Dance Party'*.

All the while Buddy was making plans with Maria for the future. They had decided to move to New York City once they were married. This, however, did not mean that he was cutting ties with Lubbock or Texas; Buddy had plans to build his own recording studio in the city, producing records for others under his new business venture, Prism Music. What it did mean was a break from Norman Petty as their producer and manager.

At the beginning of October, The Crickets headed back out on the road with the Biggest Show of Stars for 1958 tour, much reduced in length and scope on the 1957 edition. Following the conclusion of this tour the group appeared on American Bandstand to plug their latest release *'It's So Easy'*.

Following these engagements, the group made their separate ways south to Texas, with Jerry and Joe flying, while Buddy and Maria Elena drove. The group had decided that they would inform Petty of their plans to leave him on their return. Travelling by air meant that Jerry and Joe arrived home first, and then let slip their plans to leave Norman Petty. This meant he was able change their minds over splitting from his management and also relocating New York. Petty's argument was that Jerry and Joe were The Crickets, and that it was the group that were the real hit makers, not Buddy Holly.

Jerry and Joe's decision did not change Buddy's mind, nor did this setback slow him down. His life continued at a frantic pace; a recording session at New York's Pythian Temple studio in October produced four new songs, among them *'It Doesn't Matter Anymore'* and *'True Love Ways'*. This session marked a clear departure from his previous recordings, as he sang with a full orchestra instead of the band.

This new approach was directed by Buddy's concern that his latest releases were not reaching as high in the charts as before. In the US the last four releases had not made the top twenty, and even in Britain the last two releases had no entered the top twenty.

The desire to succeed, however, was still there. Buddy spent an intense period either side of Christmas at home writing and recording a batch of new songs as well as a number of cover versions of other songs. Now known as 'the apartment tapes', these eleven recordings highlight Buddy's undimmed creativity and drive to develop something new was still as strong as ever. In the weeks before Christmas he laid down demo versions of six new compositions, writing to his parents that he was particularly pleased with one of them, an answer song to 'Peggy Sue' entitled 'Peggy Sue Got Married'.

The recordings done in the new year were all cover versions and were more experimental in nature. Buddy returned to one of his earliest influences, Bo Diddley, for inspiration, recording two songs that he had written for Mickey and Silvia, 'Dearest' and 'Love is Strange'. Most interesting are his versions of Little Richard's 'Slippin' and Slidin'', particularly the two slow versions recorded at half speed so that when they played they sounded like Alvin and The Chipmunks. Despite the fact they may have been intended as a joke, these versions come across as soulful in nature, a far cry from Little Richard's almost manic delivery on the original.

The split from Norman Petty had one negative consequence, it left Buddy with a cash flow problem. All monies the Crickets had earned were channelled through Petty, as is standard in the music business. However, after being informed his services were no longer required Norman had decided to instigate a full audit of all monies to establish the full earnings of the group and who was owed what.

To address this problem, Buddy accepted an offer to headline the 'Winter Dance Party', a three-week tour of the Mid-West beginning in late January 1959. Joining him on tour as headliners were Ritchie Valens, whose latest release 'Donna' had been a number two hit in late 1958, and the Big Bopper, whose 'Chantilly Lace' was a top ten hit earlier in the year. Also on the bill were Dion and the Belmonts, who had toured with The Crickets the previous October on the back of the success of their first record 'I Wonder Why' which had been a hit the previous summer. Completing the bill was an unknown singer named Frankie Sardo.

The tour was haphazardly arranged, so the performers had to travel long distances between shows, and to make matters worse, in temperatures way below freezing. As if that was not difficult enough, the tour buses were repeatedly breaking down, often leaving the performers stranded in the middle of the cold night. Ten days into the tour Buddy had had enough, sleeping on the cold buses was a problem, while having to wait for replacement vehicles meant lengthening the already long journeys. Following the performance in Clear Lake and in order to get some sleep in a warm bed and get his stage wear laundered before the next show, Buddy decided to charter a plane for the next journey. Travelling with him that night were Ritchie Valens and The Big Bopper, both of whom were also fed up with the itinerary, the cold, the uncomfortable buses, and the constant breakdowns and wanted to try another method of transport.

As they boarded the small plane in the early hours of 3rd February 1959, the three singers were no doubt thinking of a warm night in a hotel rather than a cold night on the bus. Sadly, it was not to be. The wreckage of their plane and the bodies of its passengers were found early the next morning in a field, barely six miles from where it had taken off. All had been killed instantly.

Just over two weeks later, Coral released 'It Doesn't Matter Anymore' in Britain, which reached number one in April 1959. After his death, Buddy's British fans showed their continued dedication. Whereas in the US, his chart appearances were virtually ended by his death, in Britain the hits continued long into the next decade. Holly had left behind a wealth of unreleased recordings, which, after additional backings had been added, enabled records to be regularly released into the late-sixties.

Firstly, two volumes of greatest hits, entitled *'The Buddy Holly Story'* made the top ten of the album charts in 1959. The first years of the new decade saw a string of minor hit singles drawn from album tracks and overdubbed recordings from the six 'apartment demos' Buddy made shortly before his death.

By 1962, Norman Petty was back in the picture, enabling a further batch of releases culled from the material he held in his archives. As a result, Buddy achieved two top ten hits in 1963, just as Beatlemania had taken a hold on the country, with *'Brown Eyed Handsome Man'* reaching number three, and *'Bo Diddley'* reaching number eight. In 1963 alone, over four hundred thousand Buddy Holly singles were sold in Britain. Two hit albums were also complied from this new material, *'Reminiscing'* in 1963 and *'Showcase'* in 1964, reaching number two and three respectively.

As the original material ran out, attention turned to releasing greatest hits packages the result was that in 1978, nearly twenty years after his death, Buddy Holly reached number one on the album charts for the first time, a feat he repeated in 1993. In Britain, at least, it really was a case of not fade away.

Acknowledgements, Notes, and Sources

It is a hackneyed statement that no book is written in isolation, and this is true of this book. I'd like to thank my wife, Amanda, and Mum, Jackie, for reading through this manuscript and offering important comments and stylistic suggestions.

The material in this book also provided the basis for a 'real time' Twitter feed (@BuddyTour58) that began in February 2018 to mark the events of the tour sixty years to the day after they happened. I'd like to thank the hundreds of followers who shared this experience, the highlight of which has to be when Des O'Connor began following and messaging back! It was a lot of fun, particularly the day the blue plaque was unveiled in Salisbury, accompanied by a fantastic performance by The Bluejays (who surely must play Sheffield one of these days!).

A wealth of material exists on Buddy Holly's life and career, and I have drawn extensively on this when writing this book. Firstly, I must acknowledge a number of biographies that have provided such in depth information.

First and foremost is 'Remembering Buddy' by John Goldrosen and John Beecher. This is unsurpassed in its thorough coverage of Buddy's life and recordings. The live performance lists, recording session information, and discography are invaluable resources.

Secondly, Buddy The Biography by Phillip Norman is an excellent read, and provided a good number of quotes from members of the tour.

Another key source is Spencer Leigh's book, Everyday. He has interviewed practically everyone connected to the Buddy Holly story and the book provides a wealth of interesting quotes from a diverse range of people.

Contemporary reports of the tour were invaluable in piecing together the events described. Thanks to Keith Goodwin's close relationship with The Crickets, the NME published a good deal of first-hand accounts of the tour with direct quotes from Buddy. Also, Disc and Melody Maker both covered the tour comprehensively. Where I have drawn on these accounts, I have attributed the source in the text.

All chart information is taken from either the NME (records) or Disc magazine (juke box).

Finally, the Concerts and Package Tours Website provided an excellent overview of all concert tours that were ongoing in this period. https://www.bradfordtimeline.co.uk/mindex59g.htm

Andrew Johnston,
Sheffield, October 2018.

Endnotes

[1] John Lennon letter from 1974, published in Dawson & Leigh – Memories of Buddy Holly

[2] Background to Buddy's life is assembled from various sources, including Remembering Buddy, Buddy the Biography, and Everyday.

[3] Leigh Everyday - pg. 36

[4] According to Phillip Norman's account in Buddy the Biography - Decca at first did not realise that Buddy Holly was a member of The Crickets, and to further put them off the scent, Buddy did not sign the agreement with Brunswick Records with the other Crickets. It did eventually come to light though when Buddy came to sign his solo contract with Coral. Bob Thiele, the man who signed them to Brunswick, persuaded Decca executives that the contract had not been breeched as Buddy was still technically recording for Decca. It was decided that Buddy should be released from the clause, in return Decca would not have to pay any royalties on further releases of the first version of 'That'll Be the Day'.

[5] Jerry Allison Interview – Rave On BBC TV

[6] The information on the arrival and first night arrangements of the tour is based on Phillip Norman's account in 'Buddy the Biography' - pg. 220-221.

[7] The quotes are taken from Tim Rice's report TALKING CRICKET: That'll be the day cricket met crickets. The Daily Telegraph June 5th, 1996

[8] Background information on Ronnie Keene come primarily from his obituary in the Littlehampton Gazette August 3rd 2017
http://announcements.johnstonpress.co.uk/obituaries/littlehamptongazette-uk/obituary.aspx?pid=186272634
Background information on the other artists come from a variety of internet sources

[9] http://www.birminghammail.co.uk/whats-on/music/des-i-will-always-remember-buddy-83770

[10] Phillip Norman interview with Des O'Connor – Buddy The Biography pg. 222

[11] Phillip Norman interview with Ronnie Keene – Buddy The Biography pg. 222-226

[12] A selection of these shots can be found at
https://www.theguardian.com/music/gallery/2009/feb/02/buddy-holly-50

[13] Phillip Norman interview with Ronnie Keene – Buddy The Biography pg. 222-226

[14] Interview with Jerry Alison – Rave On, BBC TV

[15] No footage remains of this performance; the audio was preserved as someone managed to capture off-line recordings by placing the microphones of a bulky reel to reel tape recorders next to their TV speaker.

[16] TV interview with Des O'Connor 'That Sunday Night Show https://www.youtube.com/watch?v=EBxvEGAs5cs

[17] Information on the Sheffield performances is found here https://www.sheffieldtelegraph.co.uk/news/buddy-holly-legend-that-won-t-fade-away-1-450820

[18] The complete recording is available online https://www.youtube.com/watch?v=dJjEkS5lCHw

[19] Information on the visit to Longbridge comes from a report on BBC TV's The One Show 22nd October 2012 https://www.youtube.com/watch?v=thDg5Mxp-PE

[20] The photos were filed away by the BMC under the title 'Crickets Skiffle Band' – clearly nobody really had any idea who visited that day. Ibid.

[21] Background on Birmingham Town Hall is from Foster, Andy (2005). Pevsner Architectural Guides – Birmingham. New Haven: Yale University Press
Background on the performance can be found here https://www.birminghampost.co.uk/whats-on/music/50-years-death-buddy-holly-3949840

[22] All information on Pat Mace is from the following source: http://www.worcesternews.co.uk/features/mikepryce/9310103.Oh__boy__I__m_Buddy_Holly___s_mystery_girl/

[23] Des O'Connor has told this story countless times – the quote here is an amalgam of sources. Sometimes he refers to seventeen guitars, others eighteen. Sometimes he refers to a Gibson guitar and other times a Hofner. Seeing as the guitar on display is a Hofner, I have gone with that.

[24] Background on the performance in Ipswich is found here http://www.bbc.co.uk/suffolk/content/articles/2009/01/26/buddy_holly_review_bk_feature.shtml

[25] Information on the Doncaster performance is from here https://www.thornegazette.co.uk/news/late-rocker-alvin-stardust-jammed-with-buddy-holly-in-doncaster-1-6913240

[26] Background on the Wigan performance is from here https://www.wigantoday.net/news/day-buddy-put-wigan-on-the-map-1-184178

[27] Background information and quotes are from Phillip Norman – Buddy the Biography

[28] Information on the Liverpool performance is from here https://www.liverpoolecho.co.uk/news/nostalgia/the-day-the-music-lived-3455272

[29] Information on The Beatles is from the first part of Mark Lewisohn's comprehensive biography 'Tune In'

[30] Information on the Salisbury performances is from
http://www.bbc.co.uk/wiltshire/content/articles/2009/02/03/buddy_holly_salisbury_1958_feature.shtml
https://www.akemanpress.com/2017/06/15/buddy-holly-salisbury/

[31] Neil Kinnock's son, Stephen Kinnock, confirmed to me via Twitter that the rumours he attended the concert were not true.

[32] Des O'Connor sold the guitar to the Buddy Holly Educational Foundation in 2010, where it is now on display.
http://www.vintagehofner.co.uk/gallery/archtops5/arch1.html

Lightning Source UK Ltd.
Milton Keynes UK
UKHW010634070620
364508UK00001B/223

9 781788 766036